BLITZKRIEG

by

Wallace B. Black
and
Jean F. Blashfield

CRESTWOOD HOUSE
New York

Collier Macmillan Canada
Toronto

Maxwell Macmillan International Publishing Group
New York Oxford Singapore Sydney

Library of Congress Cataloging-in-Publication Data

Black, Wallace B.
    Blitzkreig / by Wallace B. Black and Jean F. Blashfield. – 1st ed.
        p.   cm. – (World War II 50th anniversary series)
    Summary: Describes the course of World War II from Hitler's invasion
of Poland up to the fall of Paris and the German occupation of France.
    ISBN 0-89686-552-5
1. World War, 1939-1945 – Campaigns – Juvenile literature. 2. World War,
1939-1945 – Germany – Juvenile literature.   [1. World War, 1939-1945.]
I. Blashfield, Jean F.   II. Title.   III. Series: Black, Wallace B. World War II
50th anniversary series.
D743.B49 1991
940.54'2 – dc20

                                                                      90-46580
                                                                          CIP

                                                                           AC

Created and produced by B & B Publishing, Inc.

Picture Credits
*National Archives - pages 8, 11, 15, 17, 23, 25, 26, 28, 29, 31, 32, 33, 37, 38 (all), 42,
    43 (all but lower left), 44 (all), 45 (upper left)*
Imperial War Museum - pages 3, 20, 21, 22, 34, 35, 36, 43 (lower left)
Polish Embassy - pages 18
United States Air Force - pages 14, 45 (all but upper left)
Steve Sullivan - Maps - pages 6, 40

CRESTWOOD   Macmillan Publishing Company   Collier Macmillan Canada, Inc.
HOUSE   866 Third Avenue   1200 Eglinton Avenue East
                  New York, NY 10022   Suite 200
                                                   Don Mills, Ontario M3C 3N1

Printed in the United States of America

First Edition

10 9 8 7 6 5 4 3 2 1

CONTENTS

1. Poland Attacked 4
2. The Road to War 7
3. Blitzkrieg–Lightning War! 13
4. The "Phony War" 19
5. War in Scandinavia 24
6. The Battle for France 29
7. Miracle at Dunkirk . . . Defeat in France...........34
A Closer Look at . . .
      Famous Leaders 43
      German Panzer Vehicles 44
      German Aircraft 45
Glossary 46
Index 47

Chapter 1

POLAND ATTACKED

It was the last day of August in 1939. A man whose name will never be known was taken from a German prison. He was given different clothes and put in a car. He was happy, because he thought he was going to be freed. Instead, he was taken to a radio station in a little village on the border between Germany and Poland. There, in front of the station, he was shot dead.

The unknown man never knew that the Germans used his body in a horrible plot. The clothes he had been given were from Poland. They were supposed to "prove" to the world that Poland had attacked Germany. The Germans who organized the plot made a radio broadcast from the station. They claimed they were being attacked by Poles.

The radio broadcast was the signal that millions of young German soldiers had been waiting for. The German army crossed the border into Poland and began to attack. It was still before dawn. The Polish people slept quietly in their beds. They had no warning of what was to come.

Germany and Poland had been arguing for years about their borders. The Polish people had hoped for a peaceful solution. But the Germans suddenly stopped arguing. Instead, they made their radio broadcast. The next morning, September 1, the huge, surprise German attack on Poland began. Blitzkrieg, which means "lightning war," came from the air, on land, and by sea. World War II had started.

Before the war ended in 1945, the warring nations fought for 2,192 days. More than 50 nations took part in World War II. The United States entered the war in December 1941 when Japan, an ally of Germany's, attacked

American territory at Pearl Harbor in the Hawaiian Islands. Eventually, over 50 million soldiers, sailors, airmen and civilians died. World War II cost the world over $1 trillion ($1,000,000,000,000).

Adolf Hitler, called *der Führer,* which means "the leader," was the chancellor, or prime minister, of Germany. He was a dictator—he had complete control of Germany. More than five months before the attack on Poland, he had told his generals that they would soon go to war.

Hitler's Germany had over 50 million people. Hitler believed that the Germans should have more *lebensraum,* (living space). He also wanted more natural resources, especially coal and iron. These things were needed to support the growing army of the Third Reich (empire), as the German government under Hitler was called. Poland, Germany's peaceful neighbor, had the space and natural resources that Hitler wanted.

Hitler's plans called for a quick victory. But his plans went far beyond Poland. Within only a few months his military forces also took over Norway, Denmark, Belgium, Holland, Luxembourg and France. His troops reached the English Channel, ready to invade and capture the British Isles. Hitler was certain that the British would ask for peace. After all, they had not gone to war when Germany took over Austria or Czechoslovakia. He was sure he would get his way again.

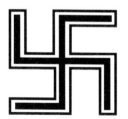

The Nazi swastika— the official emblem of Nazi Germany

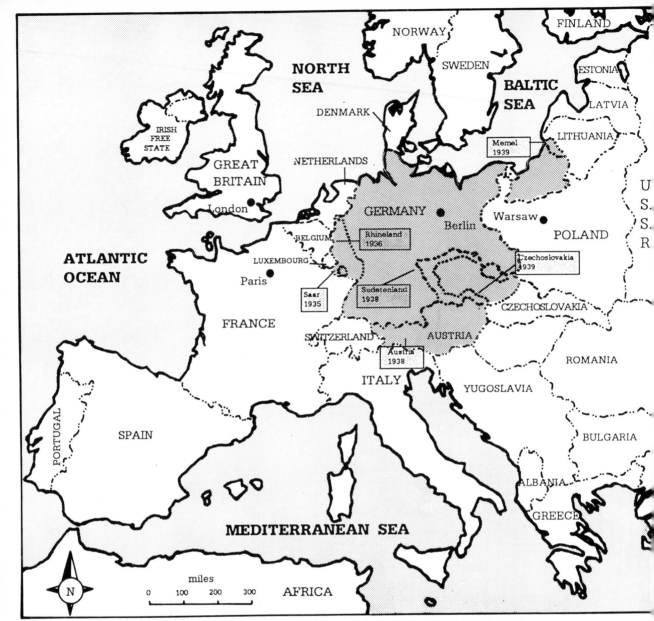

EUROPEAN LANDS ACQUIRED BY GERMANY 1935–1939

The Saar - January 1935 - France had taken over the Saar at the end of World War I. The mostly German-speaking people vote to become part of Germany once again.

The Rhineland - March 1936 - German troops take back this important region from France.

Austria - March 1938 - German troops march into Austria and proclaim that country to be part of Germany from that time on.

Sudetenland - October 1938 - Again Hitler claims a mostly German-speaking section of another country. Czechoslovakia lets the Germans take over without a fight.

Memel - March 1939 - This large, ice-free seaport was taken from Germany after World War I and made part of Lithuania. Hitler takes it back and makes it part of Germany.

Czechoslovakia - March 1939 - Hitler takes over the entire western half of Czechoslovakia. He breaks the promises he had made at Munich the previous year.

Chapter 2

THE ROAD TO WAR

The year is 1919. It is winter in Berlin, the capital of Germany. People are hungry and cold. Thousands of them are without jobs. Many businesses and factories are closed.

One year has passed since the armistice was signed on November 11, 1918. That agreement ended World War I. After almost five years of fighting, Germany was defeated by France, Great Britain, Russia, the United States and their allies. In that treaty the once-proud German nation gave up its army, much of its industry and some of its land. It also agreed not to build weapons for another war. The German people, once the richest in Europe, were now defeated, poor and hungry.

Hitler's Rise to Power

The German people saw no way to improve their lives. The nation's economy went crazy. There was no money for food, housing or clothing. It took a wheelbarrow full of paper money to pay for a loaf of bread.

The people began to listen to the words of an exciting young politician, Adolf Hitler. He convinced them that they could be great again if they would let him lead. He made great promises for a wonderful future. Hitler's popularity and his National Socialist (Nazi) political party grew. In 1933 the Nazi party took control of Germany.

Adolf Hitler was named chancellor, or head, of the German government. The *Reichstag* (the German congress) soon made him dictator. They gave him all the power he wanted. The German people wanted a strong man to lead them to greatness once again. But they failed to see the hate and madness within Hitler.

Hitler controlled the government. He also decided the way the people of Germany should live, play and think. He believed that women belonged in the home, not out working. He passed laws that kept women at home. He believed that their only concerns should be *"Kinder, Kirche, Küche"*— "Children, Church, Kitchen."

Hitler believed that his Third Reich would last one thousand years—*if* the children were taught correctly. All boys were expected to belong to the Hitler Youth. In that organization they learned to praise Hitler and take pride in being German. All their games were supposed to make them stronger and show how perfect German youth could be. When the war came, the boys were already trained to obey orders like good soldiers.

Adolf Hitler speaking to Nazi party members, soldiers and Hitler Youth

The girls had to join the League of German Girls. They learned that the most important thing they could do was be mothers. They were supposed to raise many good German children for the Reich.

Adolf Hitler was at the center of everything. He was treated like a god. No one questioned whether what Hitler wanted was right. When people met, they no longer shook hands. They raised their right arms up high and said, *"Heil Hitler!"* It means "Hail Hitler!" Children were expected to say it many times each day.

"Peaceful" Conquest

Rich lands had been taken from Germany at the end of World War I. These included the Saar, the Rhineland and the Sudetenland (see the map on page 6). Hitler wanted these lands back. He wanted their resources. And mostly German-speaking people, loyal to Germany—and to Hitler —lived there.

The Treaty of Versailles, which had been signed in 1919, had not defined the borders of Poland. The Poles were afraid that Hitler might look in their direction for more room. In 1934 he signed an agreement not to attack them.

Instead, Hitler went after the lands lost in World War I. He got them without a fight.

In early 1935 Hitler organized an election in which the people of the Saar voted to be part of Germany. The following year he declared the Rhineland also to be part of Germany. France, thinking that the German army was bigger than it was, gave up the Rhineland without a fight. Hitler had the steel plants in that region start producing heavy tanks for his armies.

Then, on March 12, 1938, the Germans marched into Austria and took control. The Austrians, Hitler said, were actually German. The other nations, especially Great Britain, feared war. To Hitler's surprise, they did not do anything to stop his "peaceful" conquests.

An important meeting was held in Munich on September 29, 1938. The people at the meeting tried to stop the German quest for more space. The leaders of four countries met and talked with Adolf Hitler. They were: Neville Chamberlain, prime minister of Great Britain; Edouard Daladier, the premier of France; Benito Mussolini, the dictator of Italy since 1925; and President Edvard Benes, who hoped to keep his country, Czechoslovakia, out of Hitler's hands.

The five leaders agreed that Austria (already part of Germany) could have 30,000 square miles of western Czechoslovakia (the Sudetenland). Hitler would have to stop demanding more lands. Hitler agreed.

Returning to England, Neville Chamberlain told the British people and the world that the meeting had been a success. There would be "peace for our time." But Hitler had lied.

Alliance with Italy

While talking peace, Germany was preparing for war. During the years leading to Hitler's rise to power, Germany was secretly rebuilding its armies. By 1934 the country was on the road to becoming a major industrial and military force once again. After Hitler came to power, he also ignored the Treaty of Versailles. To train his army and air force, he sent troops, arms and aircraft to fight in Spain's civil war. Francisco Franco was trying to take over the democratic government of Spain. Like Hitler, Franco was a fascist, a person who believes a country needs a strong, single leader. With Hitler's help, Franco won. He was the dictator of Spain until his death in 1975.

Hitler saw the big military force that Benito Mussolini, also a fascist, had built in Italy. He set out to make Mussolini and Italy friends of Germany. Starting in 1936 the two leaders signed a number of agreements that made them an "axis" of power in Europe. Later, these two countries, plus Japan, would be called the Axis powers.

A typical Nazi party parade during Hitler's rise to power

In May of 1939 the two dictators signed a "Pact of Steel." It made them military allies. However, Italy did not play any part in the early fighting in Europe. Italian forces were too busy fighting in North and East Africa.

The Persecution of the Jews

Adolf Hitler had the strong belief that true Germans were "supermen." He believed that they were a race of white, racially pure, Christian people. Called Aryan, these people were born and bred in central Europe. True Germans were called the *Volk* (folk), and Hitler was their leader, or führer. He represented authority among them. All other people—the Jews, gypsies, nonwhites, other races, criminals and the mentally ill—had no place in Hitler's plans for his "new" Germany.

Hitler had hated the Jews since his youth. He and his fellow Nazis had formed their own group of toughs. They called themselves storm troopers. They were hoodlums who ganged up on the Jews and other "undesirables." Jews were forced to give up their jobs, their businesses and their homes. Many Jews fled the country as early as 1933 when Hitler first came to power. He encouraged all Germans to consider Jews the cause of all their misery.

Some Jews, such as the great scientist Albert Einstein, came to the United States. But U.S. immigration laws would not let many Jews in. Others tried to go to Palestine, the original home of the Jews. But the British, who controlled Palestine, refused to let many in. Those Jewish immigrants who did get to Palestine eventually helped to create the nation of Israel.

On the night of November 10, 1938, Nazi storm troopers destroyed every Jewish business and home they could find. Because store windows were broken, that night came to be called *Kristallnacht,* or Crystal Night. At least 7,500 Jewish shops were destroyed and looted.

But most Jews were not able to get away from Germany. Many were made to work at hard labor or placed in prisons called concentration camps.

Chapter 3

BLITZKRIEG — LIGHTNING WAR!

Early in 1939 Hitler again told Poland that he would not attack. But then he demanded that the Poles give Germany the area called Danzig (now Gdansk). The Treaty of Versailles had left Danzig independent. Turning Hitler down, Poland went to Great Britain and France, which promised to help if war started. Hitler, angry, canceled his promise not to attack. The Poles held their breath, just waiting.

Up until that time, wars usually began with troops moving in force across known borders. First, big guns would bombard the enemy. Then ground troops would charge forward. The attacked troops would do the same thing. Battles would seesaw back and forth. Soldiers would dig trenches in the ground. They would stay there until they had a chance to attack. Armies would advance only a few miles at a time. Tens of thousands of soldiers were killed in one battle after another until a war was declared to be over.

In its surprise attack on Poland, Germany used a method of attack that had never before been seen on a large scale. Instead of trench warfare, the Germans used aircraft, tanks and troop-carrying trucks to make sudden, huge thrusts deep into the heart of enemy country. This technique came to be called blitzkrieg.

The First "Lightning War"

General Heinz Guderian, a German tank commander, studied the mistakes of World War I. He developed new ideas for using tanks to swoop into a country, supported by

Stuka dive-bombers ready to bomb Polish cities

both the aircraft and artillery. He started training tank, motorized infantry and air force units in this blitzkrieg style of warfare.

As a result, when the Germans went to war with Poland, they surprised the world. The carefully planned attack, accomplished with lightning speed, made the German army seem much more powerful than it really was.

The world quickly came to know some German terms— "Panzer," "Luftwaffe," "Wehrmacht" and "Stuka." The attack on Poland was led by high-speed panzer units of tanks and motorized guns. Panzer means "protected by armor." Stuka dive-bombers (Junkers Ju 87s), which screamed as they dove, destroyed airfields and other enemy forces on the ground. Pilots also bombed and shot at enemy troops and fleeing civilians. The Luftwaffe (German air force) bombed sleeping towns and villages as well as military targets along the line of attack. Hundreds of panzers drove with lightning speed deep into Poland. Those units of the German army (the Wehrmacht) crushed all resistance like a steamroller.

The Luftwaffe was commanded by Hermann Goering. He put over 1,400 of his best fighters and bombers into the attack. They destroyed over 600 aircraft of the Polish air force on the ground. The Polish pilots had not even known that the war had started.

The panzers bypassed Polish strong points and captured huge numbers of troops. They drove rapidly toward Warsaw, the capital of Poland. The Luftwaffe bombed and strafed (machine-gunned) from above. Tens of thousands of Polish troops were quickly surrounded and defeated.

Even the German navy (the Kriegsmarine) attacked without warning. A warship, the *Schleswig-Holstein*, had entered Polish waters during the last week of August. The ship's captain said that it was there on a peaceful training mission. But it was armed and ready for war. As the tanks rolled on September 1, the ship attacked and destroyed

German panzer unit and German infantrymen attacking a Polish village

Polish coastal forts and ships of the Polish navy. Like the pilots of the Polish air force, the sailors were taken completely by surprise.

The Poles Fight Back

Mounted on horseback like knights of old, the Polish cavalry fought bravely. But they were armed only with lances and light rifles. Thousands of men and horses of the cavalry galloped to their deaths. They were no match for the cold steel and heavy guns of the panzers and well-armed German troops.

Railroads, highways and most means of communication were destroyed by bombs and artillery fire. Towns and cities throughout the country were set on fire. Innocent civilians fled the burning cities but were left homeless and without food. Thousands of them died within the first hours of the attack.

Hitler's troops were vicious to the enemy. They regarded even little children as the enemy. The Wehrmacht wanted to win—and quickly! The horrible atrocities the Nazis would become known for began in Poland. Whole villages were set on fire and any inhabitants trying to escape were shot. People were not taken prisoner. They were shot, or stabbed, or raped and strangled. Some were even set on fire while German soldiers just stood by.

Attacked from Both Sides

Earlier in 1939 the British and the French had gone to Joseph Stalin, leader of the Soviet Union (Russia). They wanted his help in stopping Hitler. Hitler had learned that those countries were having trouble reaching an agreement. He secretly offered Stalin part of Poland to add to the Soviet Union. All the Soviets had to do in return was attack Poland from the east and promise not to fight Germany. On August 23, 1939, Germany and the Soviet Union had shocked the rest of the world with their new friendship.

During the first weeks of September the German blitz-krieg attack cut into the heart of Poland. The Polish army and civilians by the thousands retreated to the east. But then, on September 17, the Russians attacked Poland from that direction. It was a cowardly attack against a helpless nation.

The Polish people did not give up easily. Even though they were continuously bombed from the air, the people of Warsaw refused to give up. Without food, water, medical care or ammunition, they continued to fight as long as they could. They made the German soldiers pay for every street of the city they captured. Women and children fought beside the men. They built barriers, helped the wounded and attacked German soldiers.

But three weeks of nonstop war was too much. On September 27, Warsaw surrendered. More than 140,000 Polish soldiers were taken prisoner. On October 1, Hitler

German supply wagons rush past a disabled Polish tank.

Warsaw, the capital of Poland, lies in ruins.

went to Warsaw to show the world that he was in charge.

German and Russian troops and civilians moved into Poland to take over. German storm troopers and Russian secret police terrorized the people. Tens of thousands of Jews were moved into a small enclosed area of Warsaw called a ghetto. They did not have enough food or water. Disease spread quickly. Eventually the Germans would try to kill most of the Jews in both Poland and Germany.

Hundreds of thousands of other Poles were sent to labor camps and factories to work for their conquerors. The German SS (Nazi army police) controlled the western part of Poland. The Soviet Union took control of the eastern provinces. Stalin's soldiers deliberately murdered thousands of Polish military officers during the following weeks. The occupation of Poland by Germans and Russians had begun. It would last five years.

Chapter 4

THE "PHONY WAR"

Two days after the invasion of Poland, Great Britain and France declared war on Germany. Both nations were in a state of shock because their leaders had said war would not happen. But they were ready to live up to their agreement with Poland.

France and England Prepare to Fight

They immediately began to mobilize. This meant they were getting people and industries ready for war. Army reserves were called to active duty. Because poison gases had been used as weapons in World War I, gas masks were issued to civilians. The people of London and Paris expected German air raids to happen at any time. They put air-raid warning systems and anti-aircraft guns in place. Preparations for a defensive war against Hitler's Germany were under way.

France and Great Britain had been trying to modernize their armies and air forces left from World War I, but they had been working very slowly. They had thousands of planes and tanks and millions of men in their services. However, they were not ready for a modern war. The troops were poorly trained and their equipment was outdated.

France and England and their allies, Belgium and Holland, knew that the time had come for action. Hitler's military and political machine must be stopped. But how?

Hitler thought he was the greatest military genius since Napoleon. He wanted to follow up the Polish victory with immediate attacks on Belgium, Holland, Luxembourg and the coastal regions of France. Fortunately for those countries, Hitler's generals did not agree with him. Hitler listened to them. He thought the other nations would try to make peace and let him have Poland. He decided to wait.

Nothing else happened immediately. England and France calmed down. The British sent troops and equipment to France. Preparations for war were continued by both countries. But for the average "man on the street," things returned to day-to-day life as before. The people called what was happening the Phony War.

France, Great Britain, Belgium and Holland—the countries now called the Allies—spent the winter of 1939–1940 preparing for war. France called up an army of 5 million men. The British sent 390,000 men with 25,000 vehicles and supporting Royal Air Force squadrons to France.

Everyone thought this would be a "small war" and each side would ask for peace. Both sides made a few bombing runs that winter. But instead of dropping bombs, they dropped millions of pieces of paper asking for peace.

Although both sides were building their forces as fast as possible, there was no open warfare on land. It was a different story at sea.

The British ocean liner Athenia *sinking after being torpedoed by a German U-boat. This picture was probably taken from a nearby rescue vessel.*

Not as big as regular battleships, German "pocket battleships" were fast and deadly. The Graf Spee, *pictured above, and her sister ships sank dozens of Allied ships before they were driven from the Atlantic.*

The War at Sea

Lights were shining brightly and the ship's orchestra was playing. The luxury liner *Athenia* sailed from Liverpool, England, for Montreal, Canada, on September 3, 1939. The 1,100 passengers and crew gave little thought to the attack on Poland. They did not know that a U-boat (short for *untersee,* or undersea, boat) was circling nearby. Suddenly, about 9 P.M., as the passengers were dining, an explosion roared through the ship. In the darkness off the coast of Ireland, the U-boat had launched a torpedo that struck the *Athenia.*

Water poured into the ship, sending it to the bottom. That night, 112 people, including 28 Americans, died in the sea. The others were rescued by nearby ships and taken to Scotland.

Germany had struck the first blow in the Battle of the Atlantic. The attack on a civilian ship had been made without warning. The U-boat captain later said that he had thought the *Athenia* was a battle cruiser.

A German U-boat sailing calmly on the surface. U-boat "wolf packs" were deadly undersea hunters of Allied shipping throughout the war.

The British navy immediately started putting merchant (civilian passenger and freight) ships in groups called convoys. Such groups could be defended by armed escorts of the Royal Navy. Soon the convoy escorts sank several German U-boats. However, another U-boat attacked and sank the British aircraft carrier HMS *Courageous* in the North Atlantic, and 518 sailors died.

The British navy supposedly "ruled the waves," but the German navy had been growing. In addition to building a fleet of U-boats, Germany had built several large battle cruisers. The Treaty of Versailles had stopped Germany from building full-size battleships. Instead, they had built slightly smaller ships that could cruise at high speeds and carry big guns.They were called pocket battleships.

The German submarines and surface ships were sent into the Atlantic Ocean to attack British and French supply ships. The Germans also started placing mines (underwater explosives) at the entrances to British rivers and harbors. The British did the same in German waters. These underwater bombs exploded when a ship hit them. German mines destroyed about 50,000 tons of British shipping in the early months of the war. A typical merchant ship sailing in the English Channel might weigh only a few thousand tons, so that meant that 30 or 40 ships were sunk by mines in a short period of time.

Disaster at Scapa Flow

Scapa Flow, a huge British naval base hidden in the islands off northern Scotland, was thought to be safe from attack by sea. The entrance to its harbor was protected by sunken ships and submarine nets. But those traps weren't enough. On the night of October 14, the "safe" harbor was awakened by huge explosions.

In a brave and dangerous attack, the German submarine U-47 entered the heavily defended harbor. Lieutenant Commander Guenther Prien had steered his U-boat past the underwater barriers. He torpedoed the British battleship HMS *Royal Oak*. The huge ship exploded, rolled over and sank. It was a major German victory and an even greater blow to British pride.

The Royal Navy fought back in the oceans all over the world. All ships of the German navy except U-boats were forced from the Atlantic by the end of 1939. But those four months of war cost Great Britain a lot. German warships, submarines, mines and aircraft sank almost 750,000 tons of Allied naval and merchant ships during that short period.

The once mighty aircraft carrier HMS Courageous *was sunk by a German U-boat. The British had thought their aircraft carriers and battleships were safe from U-boat attacks.*

Chapter 5

WAR IN SCANDINAVIA

In the Scandinavian countries war began soon after the invasion of Poland by the Soviet Union. At first, the northern war did not have anything to do with Germany. Instead, Finland had to fight its own war with its giant neighbor, the Soviet Union.

Finland's "Winter War"

Baron Carl Gustaf Mannerheim was the commanding general of the Finnish army in 1939. He knew that war would come to Finland. However, his concern was not with Germany but with the Soviet Union. He built a line of forts across the strip of land that connects Finland with the city of Leningrad in the Soviet Union. He hoped that his "Mannerheim Line" would protect the country from the military might of the Soviet Union.

But even during the Phony War, Soviet forces were on the move. By October 10, 1939, Soviet troops had taken over Latvia, Lithuania and Estonia on their western border. Soviet leaders ordered this action to make a shield against invasion from the west. They wanted to add Finland to that shield. But the Finns knew that if their gigantic neighbor ever moved in, it would probably never leave.

On November 30, 1939, the Soviets attacked Finland. Troops swarmed across the border. Airplanes bombed Helsinki, the capital.

Greatly outnumbered in men and machines, the Finns, angry at being attacked, fought bravely. They astonished the world by their ability to fight back. Time after time

Finnish troops in camouflaged winter uniforms fought bravely against the superior forces of the Soviet Union.

throughout the cold winter months of 1939–1940, the tiny northern country turned back Soviet attacks.

In February 1940 Soviet tanks battered a hole through the Mannerheim Line. Finland was forced to ask for peace. The Finns had to accept Soviet troops in their land and give part of their territory to the Soviet Union.

The Finns had lost 25,000 men, while the U.S.S.R. had lost over 200,000 men, plus more than 600 tanks and 1,200 aircraft.

Norway and Denmark Invaded

Norway and Denmark were important to Germany. Any country that occupied Norway controlled Germany's passage from the North Sea into the North Atlantic. Germany also wanted Norway's great natural resources. Denmark's airfields and harbors were needed by Germany to support the invasion of Norway and future attacks on England.

Spring arrived in the frozen north country of Norway early in April 1940. Fishermen set out to sea. Farmers plowed their fields. The Norwegian people went on with their regular spring activities, just as they always had.

They were not aware of the traitors in their midst or the German ships about to enter their harbors. Vidkun Quisling was a Norwegian traitor who admired Hitler. He went to Berlin and convinced Hitler that the British were about to invade Norway. Many of the men around Hitler were certain that if that happened Germany could lose the war.

German infantry advance in rugged Norwegian terrain.

Great Britain had considered invading Norway to keep Germany from using that country's huge supplies of coal and iron ore. Instead, the British decided just to mine Norway's coastal waters and harbors. But British warships had not even reached Norwegian waters when ships carrying an invading army left Germany. They were disguised as coal carriers and harmless merchant ships. Weapons and troops were hidden beneath their decks. On April 9, 1940, Germany made surprise attacks on five major Norwegian seaports.

The Norwegian army fought fiercely for a time, but it was far too small to win. German troops were already hidden in Norway. Thousands more attacked both by air and from the sea. The Germans quickly overran the country.

Tiny Denmark occupies a peninsula off northern Germany. It was invaded at the same time as Norway. The helpless country quickly surrendered. However, a small "underground" force continued to fight. German telephone lines were often cut. Trucks and trains were bombed. Loyal Danes even sank the fleet of Danish navy ships so that the Germans could not use it. The Danish people continued to resist Hitler in any way possible.

The Germans did not get everything their own way. The British navy landed troops at Narvik in northern Norway. They sank or severely damaged ten German destroyers. The British troops at Narvik fought bravely, trying to retake the country. It didn't work, however, and after losing many men, the British left Norway. On June 7, the Norwegian royal family and government leaders escaped to England.

After the defeat in Norway, the British Parliament removed Neville Chamberlain as prime minister. Winston Churchill, who became the outstanding leader of Great Britain and hero of World War II, took his place. Churchill offered the people of Great Britain only "blood, toil, tears and sweat." But he promised that there would finally be victory . . . "however long and hard the road."

Junkers Ju 52 transport aircraft drop German parachute troops on a Dutch city during the attacks on Holland, Belgium and France.

Chapter 6

THE BATTLE FOR FRANCE

French and British troops gathered along the French-Belgian border. But they could not cross the border into Belgium. The Belgian government was trying to stay neutral and would not let them cross until the Germans actually attacked.

The French and British were sure that a German attack could only come through Belgium. A line of forts called the Maginot Line protected France along the French-German border.

During the 1930s the military experts in France expected the coming war to be fought in the old-fashioned way. Opposite the Maginot Line the Germans quickly built their own defenses. They called theirs the West Wall, or Siegfried Line. But it was not completely finished when the war started.

German tank traps on the Siegfried Line

Both lines of defense consisted of huge forts and supply bases connected by underground tunnels. They were defended by giant guns, tank traps, barbed wire, observation posts, and machine-gun nests. During the winter of 1939–1940, millions of men on both sides waited to fight a war they hoped would never come.

Belgium, the Netherlands (Holland) and Luxembourg stood between the German army and France. Everyone agreed that an attack on France would probably be made through these countries even though they were officially neutral. But when and where would the attack come?

The Attack through Holland

Finally, on May 9, 1940, Hitler's armies made a blitzkrieg attack into Holland. At the same time, German Stukas and Messerschmitt bombers dropped bombs on both Holland and Belgium. Silently gliders and parachute troops landed deep behind the borders of both countries.

With panzer units in the lead, the German Wehrmacht and Luftwaffe struck into the heart of Holland. The big port city of Rotterdam was firebombed and almost totally destroyed. The Dutch were forced to surrender after only five days of fighting.

Luxembourg also came under attack. It surrendered immediately.

The only place the German advance slowed down was right at the spot where Holland, Belgium and Germany meet. The huge Belgian fort called Eben-Emael was located at that point. Defended on all sides, it was known as the strongest fort in the world. Its big guns were capable of sending shells 12 miles in any direction.

On the night of May 10, a dozen German gliders slid to a stop on the undefended roof of the fort. They were silent

German troops watch Rotterdam burn after bombing.

and unseen in the darkness. A small force of German explosives experts leaped from the aircraft and raced to every corner of the fort. When the bombs they planted exploded, the guns of Eben-Emael were silenced. The panzers could now pass safely, moving on into Belgium.

The "Impassable" Ardennes

The Ardennes Forest is an area in southern Belgium filled with heavy woods and rugged hills. The Allies, thinking that it was impossible for the Germans to move through the forest, left it unprotected. But the Germans thought that their panzers and other motorized units could make it through and into France.

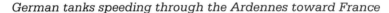

German tanks speeding through the Ardennes toward France

German infantry using rubber rafts to cross a river in France

Under the command of Field Marshal Gerd von Rundstedt, a huge German force cut its way through the Ardennes Forest. In six days the Germans completely by-passed the famed Maginot Line. Its vast forces of equipment and men were never used.

The battle in France began on May 16 when German troops stepped onto French soil at last. They quickly moved toward the English Channel. The surprise attack through the Ardennes and into France cut the British and French forces in two. The armies to the north were trapped between the German forces advancing through Belgium and Von Rundstedt's army in France attacking from their rear.

With sirens screaming, Stuka dive-bombers and other Luftwaffe fighter and bomber aircraft attacked the Allied forces without rest. Generals Erwin Rommel and Heinz Guderian led their high-speed tanks and motorized units across France. They swept aside all Allied forces in their path.

By May 21, the German army reached the English Channel. Over 500,000 British, French and Belgian troops were trapped. They retreated rapidly toward the French seaside city of Dunkirk.

Chapter 7

MIRACLE AT DUNKIRK . . . DEFEAT IN FRANCE

The defeated British and French forces continued their retreat on the roads leading to Dunkirk. Those who could walk carried their wounded friends. More than 300,000 men jammed the beaches.

Desperately, the British commanders tried to figure out how to rescue the men. Finally Prime Minister Churchill ordered Operation Dynamo, a plan for rescuing the trapped troops using navy ships.

French and British naval vessels sailed into the docks at

A French destroyer loaded with British and French troops sinking during the evacuation of Dunkirk

Allied soldiers waiting to be evacuated from Dunkirk

Dunkirk on May 26. Immediately it was clear that there were too many soldiers and too few ships.

Huge transports and other naval vessels tried to load the weary troops. But the docks at Dunkirk were small. Only a few troops could be loaded at a time. Both ships and troops were bombed and strafed by German aircraft during the slow loading process. It was a disaster!

Then suddenly a miracle happened. The pressure of the German army on the troops at Dunkirk stopped!

Hitler had won his victory. The British and French resistance had collapsed. But Hitler was afraid that his battle-weary and thinly spread army could not handle counter-attacks by the trapped troops. On May 28, he ordered the German advance toward Dunkirk to halt and reorganize. The lightning advance of the panzers was stopped.

Luftwaffe commander Hermann Goering was confident that his mighty air force could blast the men on the beaches as well as the rescue ships. But he had not counted on the skill and bravery of the pilots of the Royal Air Force. Flying from bases in England, they fought to keep the skies above Dunkirk clear of the enemy.

Civilians to the Rescue

Regular ships of the French and British navies could not handle the rescue alone. Not even the RAF could keep all Luftwaffe airplanes from trying to bomb and sink the ships as they tried to get close to shore. The British quickly realized that only smaller vessels that could sail right up to the Dunkirk beaches could rescue their troops.

In the British ports and rivers along the English Channel were thousands of commercial and amateur sailors who had their own boats. A call went out for volunteers to help with the rescue operation.

Small craft being towed on the Thames for use in the rescue at Dunkirk

British soldiers fought bravely against attacking Luftwaffe aircraft.

Soon hundreds of boats and ships of every size, shape and description were sailing to the rescue. They would come in toward the beach as far as they could. The relieved soldiers would wade out to meet them. They were soaking wet, with nothing but the clothes on their backs. The rescued were taken to larger ships waiting nearby or even all the way across the channel. Every hour saw thousands of wet, weary and wounded French and British soldiers carried to safety.

However, thousands of other Allied soldiers, sailors and civilians died on those tragic days and nights. At least 240 boats and ships were sunk. But more than 330,000 British and French soldiers were rescued.

The Allied forces had suffered a terrible defeat. But even in retreat they were victorious. The hundreds of thousands of rescued soldiers would live to return to Europe and fight again. The heroic rescue action at Dunkirk will never be forgotten.

Above—*The ceremony at which France surrendered to Germany on June 20, 1940.* Below left—*A Frenchman weeps as German troops march into Paris.* Below right—*Adolf Hitler seems to dance with glee over his conquest of France.*

France Surrenders

Half a million tons of military equipment and supplies were left on the battlefields of France. A million soldiers and civilians were captured by the Germans. The villages, towns and countryside that lay in the path of the invading German army were left in ruins. The dead and dying lined the roadsides, along with the abandoned guns, tanks, trucks and supplies of an army in flight.

On June 6, 1940, the Allied troops not trapped at Dunkirk surrendered in the north of France. To the south the final battle for France continued. There was no air force, and most means of communication had been destroyed. The remaining French and British troops could not win even though Great Britain sent some additional men and supplies.

Germany continued to control the skies over France. Air Marshal Hugh Dowding of the RAF Fighter Command refused to send more Hurricane and Spitfire squadrons to the continent. They would all be needed for the battle that he knew would soon take place over Britain. In spite of the pleas of the French and British commanders still fighting in France, Prime Minister Churchill agreed.

Italy declared war on France and Great Britain. It entered the action against them on June 10. On that same day, Paris, the capital of France, was abandoned by the French government. The Germans entered the undefended city on June 14. They kept possession of that beautiful city for almost four years.

On June 20, France surrendered to Germany. Adolf Hitler wanted to humiliate the French. He made them sign the formal surrender in the same railway car that had been used when Germany surrendered in 1918.

The Germans divided France into two parts. They occupied the northern two-thirds of the country, which included the entire western coast. The southern third of this once-

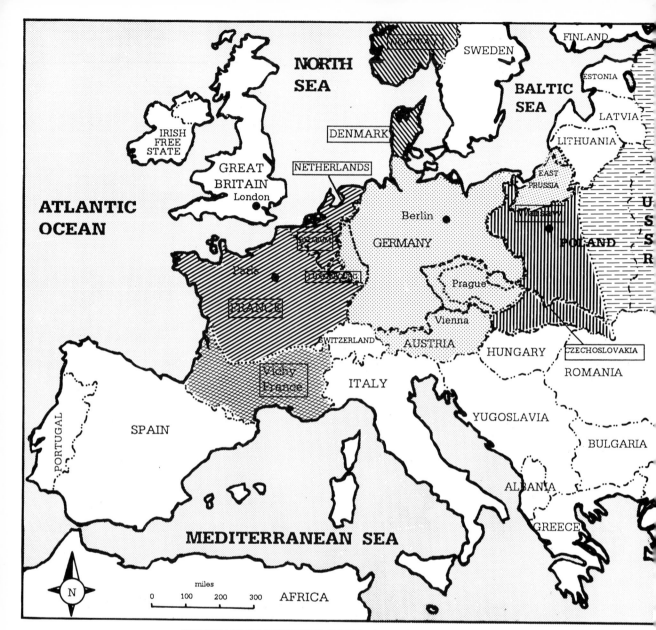

GERMAN CONQUESTS IN EUROPE IN 1939 AND 1940

In September 1939 World War II began when Germany and the Soviet Union attacked their neighbor, Poland. Denmark and Norway fell to German attacks in April and May 1940. On May 9, 1940, Hitler struck again, attacking the Netherlands, Belgium, Luxembourg and France in rapid succession. These countries surrendered by June 22, just six weeks later. The southern half of France, known as Vichy France, came under German control at the same time. Great Britain was the only country that remained to challenge Hitler's complete control of western Europe.

proud nation became Vichy France, called that because its capital was the city of Vichy. An aging French general, Marshal Henri Philippe Pétain, was made the head of this new "country." But it was still completely under German control.

German military and civilian officials poured into France. They took over and controlled all French industry, business and agriculture. They treated French men and women like slaves. They tore them from their families and put them to work in factories or in labor gangs. Most food grown in French fields was taken by the Germans to feed their own people. Food was so scarce in France that some people ate their own pets.

Soon the Jews in each of the newly occupied countries were rounded up and sent to concentration camps. Anyone who resisted was arrested. Many were shot in cold blood. Most of Europe was under the evil heel of Adolf Hitler.

Back in Great Britain, a future leader of France had risen. General Charles de Gaulle, who was to become a president of France, had escaped to England. Surrounded by other escaped French leaders, he formed a French government-in-exile. Many nations recognized it as the official government of France.

The battle for France was over. Now the British stood alone against Hitler. Only a few miles separated them from the greatest military force on earth. Hitler was asking for peace, but at the same time he was ready to carry the war to the shores of England. Under the leadership of Winston Churchill, the people of Britain refused. They would not knuckle under to an insane tyrant like Hitler. They would fight on.

The Battle of Britain was about to begin!

A German victory parade in Paris, June 1940

Famous Leaders

*Prime Minister Winston Churchill (left)
and King George VI of Britain*

*Adolf Hitler (right), chancellor of Germany,
and Benito Mussolini, dictator of Italy*

*Hermann Goering, commander
of the German Luftwaffe*

*General Heinz Guderian
developed blitzkrieg, or
"lightning" warfare.*

*General Charles de Gaulle,
exiled head of the French
government*

GERMAN PANZER VEHICLES

The Armored Car (SD-KTZ-231) (left). This was one of many six- or eight-wheeled heavily armored cars. Carried a crew of four with a 20mm cannon and a 7.92mm machine gun. Power drive and steering on all wheels made this vehicle highly maneuverable.

Half-Track Personnel Carrier (SD-KTZ-251/7) (right). This vehicle carried a crew of two plus nine troops. Other versions were used to carry supplies and were sometimes equipped with cannon and other armament.

Medium Tank (Panzerkampf-wagen Pzkw Mark III) (left) This cruising tank was the main tank of the German panzers in Poland and in the battle for France. With a crew of four, it was armed with a 37mm cannon and several machine guns.

Motorcycle with Sidecar (right) Used for scouting purposes, the vehicle was highly mobile. It was used for communications in rapidly changing battle situations. The machine gun could fire in all directions.

GERMAN AIRCRAFT

Heinkel He 111H (left) One of the main bombers of the Luftwaffe. Developed in 1935 as a transport, it was converted to carry a bomb-load of over 2,000 pounds and a crew of four with five or six machine guns.

Focke-Wulf Condor Fw 200C (right) The Condor was Germany's only successful four-engine bomber. It could carry a bomb-load of up to 11,000 pounds. Its crew of eight had up to eight cannon and machine guns. It was used mainly for locating and bombing convoys in the Atlantic Ocean.

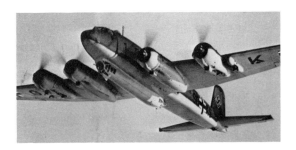

Junkers Ju 52 (left) A prewar three-engine commercial airliner, the Ju 52 was used as a bomber, troop transport, glider tug and in a variety of other ways. With a crew of three, it carried a limited bomb-load and only two or three machine guns. It could carry 16 to 18 fully armed paratroopers.

Junkers Ju 87 (right) Known as the Stuka dive-bomber, the Ju 87 was much feared by enemy ground troops. It could carry a bomb-load of up to 3,900 lbs. Two 20mm cannon fired forward and two flexible machine guns were fired by a rear gunner. It carried sirens that screamed during a dive-bombing attack.

GLOSSARY

Allies The nations that joined together during World War II to defeat Germany: Great Britain, the United States, the Soviet Union and France.

Aryan The "super-race" that Hitler and many Germans believed they belonged to.

atrocity An evil or cruel act.

Axis The partnership of Germany, Italy and Japan.

blitzkrieg Means "lightning war" in German.

chancellor The leader of a government.

concentration camp Any large prison used by the Germans to imprison Jews and other "undesirables."

fascist A person who believes that a country should have a single strong leader as a dictator.

Führer "Leader," in German. Hitler was called *der Führer.*

ghetto A part of a city where a minority group must live.

infantry Foot soldiers.

Kriegsmarine The German navy.

Lebensraum "Living space," in German.

Luftwaffe The German air force before and during WWII.

mine An underwater or underground explosive.

Nazi A person or idea belonging to the German National Socialist party.

panzer A German tank.

Phony War The six-month period following the conquest of Poland when little military action took place.

pocket battleship A high-speed, heavily armored and armed German ship slightly smaller than a battleship.

reich The German government, or empire.

Royal Air Force (RAF) The British air force.

storm troopers Nazis who acted as Hitler's private army.

strafe To machine-gun ground targets from aircraft.

swastika The four-branched emblem used by Nazi Germany.

Treaty of Versailles The treaty ending World War I.

U-boat German submarine.

Wehrmacht The German army.

INDEX

Allies 20, 32, 33, 37, 39
Ardennes Forest 32, 33
Aryan 12
Athenia 20, 21
Austria 5, 9, 10
Axis powers 10

Battle of the Atlantic 21
Battle of Britain 41
Belgium 5, 19, 20, 28, 29, 30
Benes, President Eduard 10
Berlin 7, 26
blitzkrieg 4, 13, 14, 17, 30
Britain 7, 9, 10, 12, 13, 19, 20, 22, 23,
    26, 27, 29, 30, 33, 34, 35, 36, 37,
    39, 41
British Parliament 27

Chamberlain, Neville 27
Churchill, Winston 27, 34, 39, 41, 43
concentration camps 12, 41
convoys 22
Crystal Night 12
Czechoslovakia 5, 10

Daladier, Edouard 10
Danzig 13
de Gaulle, General Charles 41, 43
Denmark 5, 26, 27
Dowding, Air Marshal Hugh 39
Dunkirk 33, 34, 35, 36, 37, 39
Dutch people 30

East Africa 11
Eben-Emael 30, 32
Einstein, Albert 12
England 10, 20, 21, 26, 36, 41
English Channel 5, 22, 33, 36
Estonia 24

fascist 10
Finland 24, 25
France 7, 9, 10, 13, 19, 20, 28, 29,
    30, 32, 33, 34, 39
Franco, Francisco 10
French 16, 22, 29, 34, 35, 36, 37, 39
Führer, der 5, 12

Gdansk 13
George VI 43
gliders 30
Goering, Hermann 15, 36, 43
Great Britain, see Britain
Guderian, General Heinz 13, 33

Hawaiian Islands 5
Helsinki 24
Hitler, Adolf 5, 7, 8, 9, 10, 11, 12, 13,
    16, 17, 19, 26, 35, 38, 39, 41, 43
HMS *Courageous* 22, 23
HMS *Royal Oak* 23
Holland 19, 20, 28, 30
Hurricane 39

Ireland 21
Israel 12
Italy 10, 11, 39

Japan 4, 10
Jews 12, 18, 41
Junkers Ju 52 28
Junkers Ju 87 14, 33

Kriegsmarine 15
Kristallnacht 12

Latvia 24
Leningrad 24
lightning war 4
Lithuania 24
Liverpool 21
London 19
Luftwaffe 14, 15, 30, 33, 36, 37
Luxembourg 19, 30

Maginot Line 29, 33
Mannerheim, Baron Carl Gustaf 24
Mannerheim Line 24, 25
Messerschmitt 30
Montreal 21
Munich 10
Mussolini, Benito 10, 43

Napoleon 19
Narvik 27

National Socialist party 7
Nazis 5, 7, 11, 12, 16
Netherlands, see Holland
North Africa 11
North Sea 26
Norway 5, 26, 27

Operation Dynamo 34

Pact of Steel 11
Palestine 12
panzers 14, 32, 35
parachute troops 30
Paris 19, 38, 39, 42
Pearl Harbor 5
Pétain, Marshal Henri Philippe 41
Phony War 19, 20, 24,
pocket battleships 21, 22
Poland 4, 5, 9, 13, 14, 15, 16, 17, 18,
    19, 20, 24
Prien, Lieutenant Commander
    Guenther 23

Quisling, Vidkun 26

Reichstag 7
Rhineland 9
Rommel, Erwin 33
Rotterdam 30, 31
Royal Air Force (RAF) 20, 36, 39
Royal Navy 23
Russia 7, 17, 18

Saar 9
Scandinavia 24
Scapa Flow 23
Schleswig-Holstein 15
Scotland 23
Siegfried Line 29
Soviet Union 16, 24, 25
Spain 10
Spitfire 39
SS (Nazi army police) 18
Stalin, Joseph 16
storm troopers 12
Stuka, see Junkers Ju 87
submarine 22, 23

Sudetenland 9, 10
swastika 5

Thames River 36
Third Reich 5, 8
Treaty of Versailles 9, 10, 13, 22

U-boat 20, 21, 22
United States 4, 7
U.S.S.R., see Soviet Union

Vichy France 41
von Rundstedt, Field Marshal
    Gerd 33, 43

Warsaw 15, 17, 18
Wehrmacht 14, 16
West Wall 29
winter war 24
World War I 7, 9, 19